# The God of Second Chances

# The God of Second Chances

TERRY W. PARKER

**Terry W. Parker**
The God of Second Chances

Published by Spines Publishing Platform
ISBN: 979-8-89383-687-5

*His Love for You*
*And*
*His Love for Me*

# Acknowledgments

First, I want to thank my Lord and Savior, Jesus Christ, who inspired me to write this book. His unwavering and unfailing love gave me a second chance to live for Him. Moreover, to my wife, Mary Ann Parker, who has been by my side every step of the way, thank you for your love, patience, and belief in me.

I thank my mother, Geraldine Black, for being a faithful prayer warrior who kept me in her prayers throughout the years. Her love and commitment to God have been an example. To my grandparents, who are now with the Lord, the Rev. Nathaniel Johnson Sr. and Rose Johnson, who played a significant role in my life. They showed me how to live Godly among ungodly people. By teaching me how to make God the focus of life.

Also, my beloved sister Teresa Michelle Parker, uncles Lavan/Bonnie, Rudy Johnson, and many others, who are also absent from the body and ever-present with the Lord. There is not a day that I do not think of you; I miss you so much and the times we shared. I will see you again when it is my turn to be called home.

# Contents

# Preface

There is no greater love when it comes to the love that God the Father has for His creation. He loved us in eternity past, and the future. However, many believers today do not grasp the unwavering and unfailing love the Lord has commanded towards us. Furthermore, God proved his love by sacrificing His only begotten Son, Jesus Christ, for all those who have repented and confessed their belief in His death, burial, resurrection, and ascension.

Inspired by the Holy Spirit, this book was written based on my short-comings and lack of trust in Jesus at my ministry beginnings. He saved me because of His love, He has never failed me, and He never will. Like so many others in the minister, when things got hard and did not go the way I planned, I got weary and walked away. I failed God and the body of Christ. Those were the darkest days of my life; I walked away from God's plan and purpose for me.

There are Christians throughout the Church who, at one point, did thank about, and some have walked away from their callings. I implore you not to give up; the Father proclaims, "For I know the plans I have for you, declares the Lord, plans to prosper you and not harm you, plans to give you hope and a future" (Jer. 29:11, New International Version). This book is written for you and me as a reminder that He is not done with us yet; we serve" The God of Second Chances."

# Chapter One

# His Love

## PART I

THE LOVE OF GOD IS UNLIKE ANY OTHER. UNLIKE THE LOVE A mother has for her children or a husband has for his wife. The love of God is unique because He is the very essence of love. Love, in biblical terms, has many Old Testament Hebrew meanings and expressions. As a result, the logos word study says one of those words is "Ahava" (אהבה). It is both a verb and a noun pinned in the (OT) 45 times. Also, the verb form "to love" is. לאהוב, the root "Aahav" is a combination of prefixes, suffixes, and vowels to create the proper grammatical word. The Hebrew meaning is "to give." (Faithlife, 1992). God revealed the ultimate love by giving us His only begotten Son, Jesus Christ.

Because God is holy and perfect, so are His laws; He gave Moses on "Mount Sinai." The Israelites, His chosen people, could not keep the law to the letter. Therefore, repeatedly they had to offer, a blood Sacrifice to atone for sins. Nevertheless, animal sacrifices by the end of the (OT) would no longer be sufficient for atonement. The people of Israel thought of themselves as Yahweh's chosen ones, and indeed they were. They became content with whatever they offered Him, believing that because of the "Abrahamic Covenant,"

God would accept their sacrifices no matter what. However, the people of Israel did not understand the sacrifices of animals offered to God, for the payment of sin was not acceptable to Him due to their attitude. The burnt offerings were ascension offerings that ascend into the presence of God. They represent the concept that one's offerings to the Lord are consumed and surrendered to Him totally. Indeed, this is where the Israelites of the (OT) failed, according to the Prophet's.

Moreover, in one of the most intense rebukes God has ever give concerning Israel, He said: Their sacrifices did not mean anything to Him. He had enough blood of bulls, lambs, and goats; God commanded them to stop bringing meaningless offerings. Hence, "Yahweh" could not even bear the assemblies; they were worthless in the eyesight of "Jehovah." The manipulating of "Elohim" was so great that He did not even receive their prayers. They became so burdensome that He could not look upon those who were praying. Also, the Lord would not listen to them" (Isa. 1:11-15).

The Israelites sacrificed and worshiped to manipulate God, they continued to live in sin because of God's promise. The New Moon and feasts were celebrated on the first day of each month (Num. 28:11-15). Instead of lifting the weight of sin from the repented offenders. The sacrifices and worship of the hypocrites became an intolerable "burden" to God. Like a sacrifice, prayer is not a device that allows sinful people to continue in sin. Instead, it is a way that a repentant worshiper communicates with a gracious God. Prayer is useless without genuine repentance. The problem is that even when they tried, the people would fail to keep His laws and commandments. Why? The answer is found in Genesis or the book of "beginnings."

The Bible tells the story of how, in the beginning, God created the world and everything in it, including humanity. The story also describes how creation is in harmony, and all is good, according to the Word of God. What happened? Adam destroyed perfect harmony between God and creation when he ate of the forbidding fruit from the tree (Gen. 3:6) after the Lord commanded him not to.

Adam was told that the day he did eat of the tree, he would die; the warning introduces death for the first time (Gen. 2:16-17). Life's creation was perfect because it obeyed God perfectly, then man's disobedience brings death, the opposite of life that God gives freely. The Apostle Paul penned, "Therefore, just as sin entered the world through one man, and death through sin, and in this way, death came to all people, because all sinned." (Rom. 5:12).

This passage compares "just as; and so also" in vs. (12-21). Adam and Christ are each critical figures in redemptive history. Both have acts that have ultimate significance for all whom they represent. Adam brought death and condemnation to all humans, which is more than made up for by Christ's obedience, which brings righteousness and life to all who receive God's gracious gift. The one righteous act of Christ's death brings justification and life to all people; this is the ultimate example of God's love for His children. The new covenant empathetically promises complete and eternal forgiveness, which the Mosaic order could not accomplish, but Jesus Christ has provided in full according to Scripture (Eph 1:7, Matt 26:28, Acts 2:38, 10:43, Rom 4:7-8, Rev 21:4).

# *His Love Is Unwavering*

BECAUSE THE SINS OF MAN WHERE SO GREAT AS THEY WERE
pre-flood (Gen. 6:5-8) by the end of the (OT) God did not communicate
with humanity for over 400 years. No canonical books are written around
this time between the testaments which are called by some Scholars "the
silent years." Nevertheless, many significant historical, social, and religious
activities occurred during these four centuries. God the Father did not
stop loving His people during this period the redemptive plan for
humankind had already been in place before the creation. Moreover, the
unwavering love of God will stand because He promised.

Furthermore, "The study of God's nature should be seen as a means to
a more accurate understanding of him and hence a closer personal relationship with him." (Erickson 2013, 235). There are four words used for
the word Love. "Godly Love (Gr. agape), sexual Love (Gr. eros), brotherly
Love (Gr. Philips), or the affection parents have for children, vassals for
rulers, or the Love of dogs for their masters (Gr. storge)" (Graves 2018,
102).

The Lord promised Abraham, and the calling of Abram in Genesis
marks the beginning of God's relationship with the father of faith. The
scene was set in (Gen. 11:27-32) the promise will influence both Abrams

immediate future and long-term future of all humankind (Gen. 12:1-3). Because God's love is "unwavering," His invitation to Abram is critical throughout the book of Genesis. Abram is now at the heart of God's plans to reverse all that has gone wrong since the Garden of Eden (Gen. 3:22-24). The theme of God's blessing others through Abram later links to the line of descendants traced initially through Isaac and Jacob (22:18; 26:4; 27:29; 28:14).

In the (NT) the Apostle Paul sees in this promise of blessings as an advance announcement of the gospel (Gal. 3:8), the blessing coming through Jesus Christ, the seed of Abraham (Gal. 3:16 and Gen. 22:18). Likewise, the Apostle Peter associates Jesus Christ with the fulfillment of God's promise to bless the families of the earth (Acts. 3:25-26). Furthermore, although the initial promise of nationhood and international blessing is conditional upon Abram's obedience, because of His unweaving love for his children, God the Father later guarantees these by making two covenants with Abram in (chapter 15 and 17).

First chapter 15 promises that Abram's descendants will be as numerous as the stars in the sky (Gen. 15:5). Then God told Abram that his descendants would take possession of the land of Canaan (Gen. 15:7). Chapter seventeen is where God makes the second covenant with Abram. The Covenant of Circumcision and changed his name from Abram to Abraham meaning "father of a multitude."

The covenant in Chapter seventeen involves the birth of Abraham's son, with whom God will establish the covenant in the next generation. This covenant is God's promise to bless the nations of the earth (Gen.12:3), which the change of Abram's name to Abraham reflects. God's speech to Abraham moves from God's part (Verse. 4-8) to that of Abraham (Verse. 9-14) and then to Sarah (Verse. 15-16). Moreover, "God Almighty" because of His "unwavering love" introduces Himself to Abram as "El Shaddai." or "God All-Sufficient" He is sufficient and will fulfill all the promises He has made to Abraham and His descendants that also includes you and me as all nations.

That attitude of love cherishes the wrongdoer as a friend to be won, not as an enemy. Unwavering love covers over and protects the wrongdoer. In the meantime, the one who is love draws a veil over all wrong no matter how many and however bad displays that love compassionately. God forgive the Israelites for their failure to keep the law and do right before Him. Although they would endure captivity by the Babylonians, Assyrians, Persia, and Romans, God the Father would not forget His promise. Instead, He would confirm the promises through Abraham, Isaac, and Jacob. Three patriarchs would be influential figures in Judaism, Christianity, and Islam because of God's unwavering love for humanity.

# His Love Is Unfailing

THE FATHER'S LOVE IS UNFAILING IN THIS WAY, JESUS BEING raised up on the cross and His glorious exaltation is grounded in God's love because He gave His Son for those whom He chose (Rom. 8:29-30). Hence, God's love is unselfish and costly, unlike how sinners selfishly love the world by conforming to it (1 John. 2:15-17). Likewise, God demonstrates His love for us at His set time by sending His Son to die on our behalf. Scripture says, "You see, at just the right time, when we were still powerless, Christ died for the ungodly." (Rom. 5:6).

The Psalmist proclaimed, "How priceless is your unfailing love, O God! People take refuge in the shadow of your wings." (Ps. 36:7). The Psalmist calls His love more priceless than any other attribute. Why? Because without His unfailing love, the other attributes would be meaningless. As a result, men can put their trust in the Lord, and He will not fail them. Also, God's unfailing love is who He is; according to John, "Whoever does not love does not know God, because God is love." (1 John. 4:8).

In the book of Romans, the 8th chapter, nowhere can the apostle Paul find anything in the whole universe of God that can sever the relationship that the children of God have with their Father's love. Likewise, out of this love springs life through the Spirit, which the believer benefits from Christ's death as He liberates us from the power of sin and death. Also, the Spirit conquers the flesh, allowing God's children to conform to His will as we are drawn to His love.

His Love is Unmerited

The Father Sovereignly sets His "Unmerited Love" on undeserving people in the book of Malach and on believers today. Malach preached to those who doubted God (1:2-3), the cynics (1:7, 2:2), the cold-hearted (2:16), cheaters (3:5), people who were indifferent (3:14-15), the faithful (3:16-17), and the openly wicked (4:1). The theological theme is that God is a Covenant-maker who loves and has chosen Israel to be His people. However, the Israelites break the Covenant through their doubt, blemished sacrifices, divorce, injustice, and withholding tithes. Nevertheless, God would once again demonstrate His "Unmerited Love" for those who remain faithful and renew His Covenant.

As a result, because of the Covenant, the redeemed can be assured when believers come to God with repentance, hearts for Him, and a ministry of reconciliation that we are reconciled to Him through Christ. According to the apostle Paul, the Father's grace is unmerited favor; it is the basis and cause of salvation (Rom. 3:24, 11:6, Titus. 3:7). Consequently, it is God's unmerited favor towards those who have transgressed His commandments and deserve His wrath.

However, humankind could not help itself because they are "dead in transgressions" (Eph. 2:5). Above all, faith is a gift from God; it is the human response by which sinners receive God's salvation. As a rule, it is a confident trust in God whereby believers refuse to justify themselves based on their achievements but gratefully receive what God has already accomplished in Christ.

# His Love Is Unmerited

THE FATHER SOVEREIGNLY SETS HIS "UNMERITED LOVE" ON undeserving people in the book of Malach and on believers today. Malach preached to those who doubted God (1:2-3), the cynics (1:7, 2:2), the cold-hearted (2:16), cheaters (3:5), people who were indifferent (3:14-15), the faithful (3:16-17), and the openly wicked (4:1). The theological theme is that God is a Covenant-maker who loves and has chosen Israel to be His people. However, the Israelites break the Covenant through their doubt, blemished sacrifices, divorce, injustice, and withholding tithes. Nevertheless, God would once again demonstrate His "Unmerited Love" for those who remain faithful and renew His Covenant.

As a result, because of the Covenant, the redeemed can be assured when believers come to God with repentance, hearts for Him, and a ministry of reconciliation that we are reconciled to Him through Christ. According to the apostle Paul, the Father's grace is unmerited favor; it is the basis and cause of salvation (Rom. 3:24, 11:6, Titus. 3:7). Consequently, it is God's unmerited favor towards those who have transgressed His commandments and deserve His wrath.

However, humankind could not help itself because they are "dead in transgressions" (Eph. 2:5). Above all, faith is a gift from God; it is the human response by which sinners receive God's salvation. As a rule, it is a confident trust in God whereby believers refuse to justify themselves based on their achievements but gratefully receive what God has already accomplished in Christ.

# His Love Is Unconditional

IN THE SEVENTH CHAPTER OF DEUTERONOMY, GOD MAKES A covenant with His people to demonstrate His unconditional love for them so that all His promises are fulfilled. The Father's identity is not in doubt; He is the God of faithful love for "a thousand generations" of those who follow Him (vs. 9). God's motive for choosing Israel is love, and the Lord wants His children to love Him back. However, the Israelites came up short, observing the Law with a willing spirit. Hence, gratitude is the least remembered of all virtues, and the Israelites were exposed to the danger of forgetfulness.

Nevertheless, God has no higher commandment than love, He, who loves His people "with an everlasting love" (Jer 31:3). God's unconditional love is (Agape) because it is selfless and sacrificial. Likewise, God's working for Israel in the future is possible only because He can pardon sin and not allow it to deter Him from His future program. The Father is occupied with fulfilling all that He covenanted to Israel in His unconditional covenant given to them and because of His Word and for His glory.

Moreover, when God could find no justification for showing mercy to Israel, He seized the opportunity to display His unconditional love again by saving Israel at the Red Sea (Psalm 106:7-10). The Lord remembers His covenant promises or faithfulness, derived from the same word translated as "love" (hesed), and connotes the Lord's faithfulness to His promises.

# His Love Is Unchanging

SCRIPTURE DECLARES THAT GOD'S LOVE IS UNCHANGING; THE author of the letter to the Hebrews penned, "Jesus Christ is the same yesterday and today and forever" (Heb 13:8). The declaration is a significant Christological phrase that links (vs. 7). Also, because the Son is the Creator of the heavens and earth, He will remain the same when all creation changes (Heb 12:26-27). Moreover, His "years will never end" (Heb 1:12); the Son's eternal existence is foundational to His abiding priesthood, and its effects on all believers are unchanging.

Likewise, "As the Logos, he is the light that has enlightened everyone coming into the world; thus, in a sense, all truth has come from and through him (John 1:9)" without change. Hence, God says, "I the Lord do not change" (Mal 3:6), indirectly a theological commentary on the nature of God's being. The Father's Holy character and eternal purposes are immutable; God is not static in His actions. Indeed, the statement affirms God's integrity as a covenant maker and His faithfulness as a covenant keeper with His children.

In addition, "every good and perfect gift is from above, coming down from the Father of the heavenly lights, who does not change like shifting shadows" (James 1:17). God's gifts are helpful, practical, and perfect, lacking nothing. The Lord is always consistent; He does not embrace changing His nature. The Psalmist proclaims, "But you remain the same, and your years will never end" (Psalms 102:27). The passage points to Jesus, the incarnate Son of God and Creator of the universe, who will never change to the glory of God!

# Chapter Two

# *His Love*

## ∾

### PART II

The love of God also extends equally to women in the Bible; throughout history, they have played a significant role in God's redemptive plan concerning humanity. We will examine the lives of some of these women and how they have helped shape the landscape of God's plan for His chosen people, the Jews, and the Church. "Because He is no respecter of person or sex, He used and still uses women to accomplish His beneficent ministry in a world of need" (Lockyer 1988, 9).

Women such as Sarah, Rebecca, Ruth/Naomi, Rahab, Esther, and Mary all were faced with decisions that were made that would change their lives forever, and their names would go into the pages of history because they each, in the end, believed and trusted in the God of love who keeps His covenant promises. For example, in (Gen. 11:29) we are introduced to "Sarai," whose name God changes to "Sarah" in (Gen. 17:15); her inability to have children is a significant obstacle to the fulfillment of God's promise that Abram will have many descendants and become a great nation (Gen. 12:2). Moreover, the same problem recurs with Rebekah (Gen. 25:21).

However, in each case, God enables them to conceive a son to be born, who becomes an essential link in the unique and intriguingfamily line traced throughout Genesis and the Bible. These stories are a Testament to the lengths that God will go to demonstrate His love and the courage of the women He chose before the foundation of the world to play their part in His plan to reconcile His people back unto Himself.

# Sarah

According to Scripture, Sarah, wife of Abraham, was also his half-sister on his father Terah's side (Gen. 20:12). Also, she was ten years younger than Abraham, and they married in Ur of the Chaldeans (Gen. 11:31) when Abraham and Sarah left Ur for Haran, she was about sixty-five years old. The story goes that after their encounter with the Egyptians and Abimelech King of Gerar (Gen. 20:1-18), some years later, Sarah was still without a child at the age of seventy-five. She began to lose hope of producing an heir for Abraham.

Therefore, Sarah convinced Abraham to take her handmaid, Hagar, as a concubine, a custom referred to in a few ancient Near Eastern texts. Hagar, in this context, serves as a surrogate for Sarah, a common practice in the ancient world. Sarah relied on others and their traditions instead of trusting God and waiting on Him (Gen. 16:1-16). Indeed, Hagar conceived a son, but he would not be the heir God promised, for he was not one of Sarah and Abraham's offspring.

In addition, "When God changes Abram and Sarai's names, He adds the letter hey (as there are two hey in Yahweh) to each of their names to make "Abraham" and "Sarah," which signifies that the Spirit of God is within the mother and father of Judaism" (Whittock and Whittock 2021,

23). As a result, because of His love and promises, and despite Sarah's lack of faith, God does what they had considered impossible in her old age at 90: she conceives a son, Isaac (Gen. 21:1-7). This story reminds all women that no matter how old you are, God's love is ageless, and God is not done with you yet!

# Rebekah

THE STORY OF REBEKAH, THE ACCOUNT OF REBEKAH becoming Isaac's wife not only underlines how God providentially directs Abraham's servant to her but also portrays Rebekah as following in Abraham's footsteps by leaving her family and country to settle permanently in Canaan. She was the daughter of Bethuel, Abraham's nephew (Gen. 22:23), and the mother of Esau and Jacob. Rebekah had no children, although she had been married for twenty years, a story that echoes the challenges faced by Sarah. Only a woman knows the pain, disappointment, and embarrassment she must have endured throughout her marriage.

However, God would answer Isaac's prayer and give her twins (Gen. 25:20-26); her experience while carrying the boys foreshadowed the conflict between her descendants, and she was told God had chosen the younger twin for His blessing. Nearing death, Rebekah, a key player in God's plan, overhears Isaac speaking to Esau, and she both instigates and oversees Jacob's deception of Isaac. However, when Jacob voices anxiety about Isaac finding out, Rebekah states she will bear full responsibility (Gen. 27:5-13).

Therefore, Isaac unknowingly blesses Jacob instead of Esau; nevertheless, despite Rebekah's deception, Jacob experiences two encounters with God that transform his understanding of God and are part of how God changes him (Gen. 28:10-22). Because Rebekah left her homeland to be with His chosen people, "God rewarded her faithfulness by including her in His family, His people of promise. She became one of the ancestors of Jesus, the ultimate expression of God's faithful love" (Rubio and Williams 2023, 31).

# Ruth/Naomi

THE BOOK OF RUTH, FEATURING TWO ORDINARY WOMEN IN A small town, asserts that God providentially appointed David and his descendants to rule Israel. Moreover, Ruth the Moabite's exemplary character may seek to answer widespread criticism about the many foreign advisors whom Solomon had brought into the country to help organize his Kingdom. Above all, the purpose of Ruth is to praise God's sovereignty, the loyal protection of His people, and His desire for them to flourish as a nation. A significant theme of the book is that it pleases God (Yahweh) when Israel welcomes foreigners who, whatever their past, worship Him, a message that enlightens and inspires.

Two theological beliefs shape the book: (1) Yahweh's sovereign activity is ongoing but hidden, and (2) Yahweh plays a cosmic role as a doer and rewarder of hesed (acts of loyalty, compassion, mercy). The book opens with sadness because Naomi loses her husband and sons and becomes a childless widow in a land where the Judges rule and there is a famine (Ruth. 1:1-5). She tries to persuade the two young widows of her sons to return to Moab rather than accompany her to Bethlehem, and Orpah obeys and returns (vs. 14).

Naomi is postmenopausal, so the younger women are foolish to stick with her; she cannot provide them with new husbands to replace her dead sons (Ruth. 1:11-15). However, Ruth renounces her ties to Moab to embrace Naomi's country, family, and faith in Bethlehem. By divine appointment, she meets Boaz, her future husband, and Naomi gains a guarding redeemer. The two will go on to have a son, and they called him Obed, meaning "one who works/serves." Obed, "Was the father of Jesse, the father of David" (Ruth. 4:16-17), whom Jesus descends.

# Rahab

THE STORY OF RAHAB IS FOUND IN THE BOOK OF JOSHUA, A story of faith that changed history. She was a prostitute of Jericho, a Canaanite woman. Whose house two spies stayed just prior to the conquest of Palestine by Joshua (Josh. 2:1-21). Scripture tells us that Rahab was terrified by the approach of the Israelites; therefore, she agreed with the spies to protect them if they would guarantee the safety of her family and herself. Rahab risks her life to hide the spies and confesses her faith in God's acts of redemption (Josh. 2:9-11).

Doing so, Rahab separated herself from Jericho's people and identified with Israel, beginning the longest biblical prose speech by a woman; it went like this: "I know The Lord has given you this land, a great fear of you has fallen on us, all who live in this country are melting in fear because of you (vs. 9). "We heard, how the Lord dried up the water of the Red Sea, what you did to Sihon and Og (vs. 10). "When we heard it, our hearts melted in fear, everyone's courage failed because of you, for the Lord your God is God in heaven above and on the earth below" (vs. 11).

Rahab concealed the spies from the agents of the King of Jericho and helped them to escape through her window on the city wall. As a result, at the fall of Jericho, Joshua spared Rahab and her relatives (Josh. 6:17, 22,

25). According to Matthew's genealogy of Jesus Christ, Rahab became the wife of Salmon and the mother of Boaz (Matt. 1:5). The author of Hebrews cites her as an example of faith (Heb. 11:31). James refers to her demonstration of faith by good works (Jas. 2:25). Indeed, all women should be encouraged by this woman who society deemed an outcast, however; the God of second chances forever changed her life and that of her family, Hallelujah!

# Esther

ONE OF THE MOST POPULAR BOOKS AMONG WOMEN, THE STORY of Esther and Mordecai is a literary masterpiece with profound theology. Indeed, God fulfills His redemptive promises through great miracles and divine providence working through ordinary people and events. Further, even the actions of people who do not worship Him are woven into patterns and purposes determined by the sovereign Lord alone. The book of Esther affirms that God is still faithful to the covenant promises He made at Sinai and that those living beyond the borders of the promised land are not beyond the reach of His redemptive protection.

Mordecai, Esther's cousin, a minor official of the palace, raised her as his daughter. Xerxes, the Persian King, had divorced his wife Vashti, and when he sought a new queen from among the maidens of the realm, he chose Esther as his queen (Est. 2:1-17). In the meantime, Mordecai uncovers a conspiracy to kill the King, reports it, and he is giving credit (Est. 2:21-23). However, the King honored Haman the Agagite, but Mordecai would not kneel to give honor to him (Est. 3:1-4). Whether it was personal resentment, political enmity, or religious conviction, Mordecai's decision set life-threatening consequences for his people into motion.

For this reason, Haman plots to destroy the Jews because Persia ruled such a vast area, including Judah and Jerusalem; this plot threatened to annihilate all God's covenant people. Because of her favor with King Xerxes Mordecai, persuades Esther to help; this is the defining moment in Esther's life that makes her a prime example of faithfulness to God that women of God must imitate. Esther calls for a three-day fast; she recognizes that she is caught up in something much bigger than her own life (Est. 4:15-17).

Mordecai reminds Esther of the unusual circumstances that placed her in the position she holds and asks her to consider that it has been for this very reason that she intervened to save the Jewish nation at this moment in history. Queen Esther takes charge and brings her request to the King, a banquet for the King and Haman (Est. 5:1-7). Nevertheless, when Haman leaves the palace, Mordecai refuses to bow in his presence, which enrages Haman, and he sets up a pole to impel Haman on (vs. 9-14).

However, the outcome is reversed, and Mordecai is honored and commemorated by the annual festival of Purim. The full extent of Haman's tragic miscalculation begins to unfold, and Haman's wife and advisors announce the victory of God's people against all odds (Est. 6:13). Esther cleverly plays her hand as she reveals her identity to the King by inciting him to ask her a question she cannot refuse to answer. Haman is the one! Moreover, Haman cannot deny what the King already knows. Esther's accusations of Haman send Xerxes into an enraged quandary, and finally, the pole Haman set up for Mordecai ironically becomes Haman's end (Est. 7:9).

Esther, the daughter of Abihail (Est. 9:29), rose to the throne of Persia through providential circumstances. Her Story is not just a historical account but a powerful example of how God can intervene in our lives. Her courage and faith allowed God to intervene for His people in their time of need because of His love. This same God is ready and able to intervene in your life, just as He did for Esther.

# Mary

A<small>CCORDING</small> <small>TO</small> S<small>CRIPTURE</small>, M<small>ARY</small> <small>HAS</small> <small>A</small> <small>UNIQUE</small> <small>ROLE</small> <small>IN</small> God's plan of redemption (Gen. 26:24, 28:15, Exod. 3:12, Judg. 6:12). The angel Gabriel appears to her, which demonstrates that God is fulfilling His ancient prophecies and signifies the climax of the history of salvation (Luke. 1:19), Gabriel only other appearance is in (Dan. 8:16, 9:21), in the (OT). In his greeting he tells Mary she is "Highly Favored! The Lord is with you" (Luke. 1:28). "You will conceive and give birth to a son call Him Jesus" (Luke. 1:31). "He will be great and will be called the Son of the Most High. The Lord will give Him the throne of His Father David, and He will reign over Jacob's descendants forever, His Kingdom will never end" (Luke. 1:32-33).

When Mary visited Elizabeth, she blessed Mary by proclaiming, "Blessed are you among women, and blessed is the child you will bear!" (Luke. 1:43). For this reason, Mary sang a song and based on its opening word in the Latin Vulgate, this song is known as the Magnificat ("glorifies"), (Luke. 1:46-56). Further, Mary's experience is personal and reflects the reversal of fortunes that people will experience through her son (vs. 52-55). Moreover, this song's themes and language resemble Hannah's song (1 Sam. 2:1-10); both foreshadow God's acts of deliverance.

Just like Mary, we are to devote our minds to the truth of God" (DiMarco and Youngman 2017, 46). When Jesus prayed for His Disciples, He prayed to the Father that He would "Sanctify them by the truth; your word is truth," Jesus proclaimed (John. 17:17). This revealed truth is now embodied in the Bible, the Word of God. He gave us this truth because of His love for you and me.

# Chapter Three

# His Love

## PART III

In this chapter, we will discuss one of the most important storylines in the (NT), the redefinition of the people of God because of His love. For example, in the (OT) the people of God are identified by their descent from Abraham: the people of Israel. Also, the (OT) indicates that God's people cannot ultimately be confined to Israel. However, the (NT) announces a new and revolutionary step in this direction. The people of God are now defined by their relationship to Jesus Christ, the descendant of Abraham.

Moreover, the transformative power of the New Covenant is a source of hope and inspiration for believers. Only Jews who place their faith in Christ are actual people of God, and Gentiles, through that same faith, can now join believing Jews as full and equal members of God's people. This 'New Covenant' has been inaugurated through the redemption won by Christ's shedding of His blood on Calvary. The pouring out of God's Spirit with new power on all His people is a seal of this transformation— consequently, the men who wrote the (NT) letters certainly dealt with trials and tribulations, but they did so with the hope and inspiration that the New Covenant brings.

Men Christ called to usher in the church age, such as Peter, Paul,

James, and John, played a vital role in what is now called the (NT). Their contributions to Christianity will be forever cemented and serve as a powerful reminder that God can and will use us, regardless of our background or social status. And when we fall short, we can take comfort in knowing that we serve a faithful God who offers us second chances, encouraging us to keep moving forward in our faith journey.

# Peter

According to the Scriptures, Peter was a native of Bethsaida (John. 1:44), the son of a confident John (1:42, 21:15-17, called Jonah in Matt. 16:17). The evaluation by the Sanhedrin of Peter and John was one of "unschooled, ordinary men" (Acts. 4:13). Peter and his brother Andrew were fishermen on the Sea of Galilee, he was a married man (Mark. 1:30, 1 Cor. 9:5) and at the time of Christ's Galilean ministry lived in Capernaum (Mark. 1:21,29). Peter and Andrew, along with James and John, were called by Jesus to have a full-time association with Him and to be trained as "fishers of men" (Mark 1:16-20, Luke 5:1-11).

Peter was one of the most beloved and wholesome members of the apostles. He was eager, impulsive, energetic, self-confident, and daring, yet at times he was unstable, fickle, weak, and even cowardly. For instance, after Jesus was arrested, Peter denied knowing Him three times (Matthew 26:69-74, Mark 14:66-72, Luke 22:55-62, John 18:15-18). However, after great sorrow and repentance, Peter "went outside and wept bitterly" (Matthew 26:75). Following Christ's resurrection and ascension, Peter addressed the crowd on Pentecost. The coming of the Holy Spirit at Pentecost marks the start of the new covenant and the promised end-time coming of the Spirit (Joel 2:28-32, Isaiah 32:15, Jeremiah 31:33-34, Ezekiel 36:26-27).

This also marks the beginning of the church, which becomes a fellowship of unity, support, power, and witness for Jesus Christ; "about three thousand were added to their number that day" (Acts 2:41). Moreover, Peter wrote two letters in the New Testament, 1 and 2 Peter. His story is an inspiration for all who feel they have failed Christ at one point or another in ministry. It also reminds us that Christ is with us "always to the very end of the age" (Matthew 28:20).

# Paul

THE APOSTLE PAUL'S HEBREW NAME WAS SAUL (ACTS. 13:9); the change to the Greek name was particularly appropriate when the apostle began his leadership position in bringing the gospel to the Gentile world. Also, "Saul, like Jesus and His disciples, was a Jew, and he first made his name by persecuting Christ's followers" (Sampley 2016, X). The apostle was a tentmaker by trade (Acts. 18:3); he grew up near the busy Greco-Roman city of Tarsus. Further, it should be noted that he was a Roman citizen (Acts. 22:28). Later, in his ministry, his Gentile connections greatly aided him in bridging the chasm between the Gentile and the Jew.

Saul was sent to Jerusalem at the proper age and completed his studies under the famous Gamaliel (Acts. 22:3, 26:4-5). He was a superior, zealous student (Gal. 1:14) who absorbed the teaching of the (OT) and the rabbinical learning of the scholars. His active opposition to Christianity marked him as the natural leader of the persecution that arose after the death of Stephen (Acts. 7:58-8:3, 9:1-2). Saul's unwavering conviction that Christians were heretics and that the honor of the Lord demanded their extermination (Acts. 26:9) was a testament to the intensity of his beliefs, although unmerited.

According to Scripture, he was on his way to Damascus, armed with authority from the high priest, when he encountered the risen Christ (Acts. 9:1-19, 22:6-16, 26:12-23). His radical transformation from persecutor to apostle is essential for the narrative of Acts and the history of Christianity. Now known as Paul, he is responsible for at least 13 (NT) letters. Therefore, it is no secret that his unique career, marked by his fervent nature, is a testament to his intense commitment to Christ and an example to you and me that we serve the God of second chances!

# James

James, the brother of Jesus, is mentioned twice in the Gospels with his brothers Joseph, Simon, and Judas (Matt. 13:55, Mark. 6:3). However, it must be noted that James was not a follower of Christ, his brother during His earthly ministry (John. 7:5). Likewise, there is no specific mention of his conversion; it is said that the resurrected Christ appeared to him after the resurrection (1 Cor. 15:7), which would explain why? James became a disciple of Christ after His death. Nevertheless, it is interesting that sometime later, James became the leader of the Jerusalem church (Acts. 12:17, 15:13, 21:18, Gal. 1:19, 2:9), meaning that the encounter radically changed him.

According to early church tradition, James was appointed the first bishop of Jerusalem by the Lord Himself and the apostles. He presided over the first Council of Jerusalem, a significant event called to consider the terms of admission of Gentiles into the Christian church. James's influence, and respect among his colleagues were evident as he may have formulated the decree that met with the approval of all and was circulated to the churches of Antioch, Syria, and Cilicia (Acts. 15:19-29).

James's excellent name, even among Jews, earned him the title "James the Just" according to Jewish and Christian traditions. He is also responsible for one letter: "In a few pages, it offers concrete counsel on an array of issues that confront Christians daily: trials, poverty, materialism, pride, favoritism, justice, planning, prayer, illness, and more" (Nielson and Doriani 2019, 8). It is essential to remember that the power of God transformed James. This is the same transformative power of God's word that calls you and me to be listeners and doers of His word, inspiring hope and faith in our hearts towards the God who is love!

# John

THE APOSTLE JOHN WAS THE SON OF ZEBEDEE AND BROTHER OF James, the apostle, who was put to death by Herod Agrippa I (Matt. 4:21, Acts. 12:1-2). John and his brother James were fishermen on the Sea of Galilee (Mark. 1:19-20). He is the first to be introduced as a disciple of John the Baptist's call to repentance and baptism in preparation for the coming of the Messiah. John was introduced to Jesus by John the Baptist, when he proclaimed, "Look, the Lamb of God!" (John. 1:36). John and Andrew, Simon Peter's brother followed Christ that day, and their lives would be forever changed.

John was one of the three apostles closest to Jesus, the other two being Peter and James, John's brother. The Gospels make it clear that Christ greatly loved him. The apostle was also present at the Transfiguration of Jesus (Matt. 17:1, Mark. 9:2, Luke. 9:28). At the Passover feast John lay close to the breast of Jesus and asked who His betrayer would be (John. 13:25). However, when Jesus was arrested, John fled, as did the other apostles (Matt. 26:56), but before long he recovered enough courage to be present at the trial of Jesus along with Peter (John. 18:16).

Five books of the (NT) are attributed to him: the fourth gospel, Three Letters, and Revelation. Indeed, it is evident from Scripture that John was one of the greatest of the apostles. He is described as the disciple Jesus loved, no doubt because of his understanding and love for his lord. Also, the defects of character with which he began his career as an apostle, undue vehemence, intolerance, and selfish ambition, all went away when he encountered his resurrected lord, as he became known for his gentleness and kindly love traits you and me also must have.

# Chapter Four

# His Love for You

THE LOVE OF GOD FOR YOU, AS REVEALED IN SCRIPTURE, "HAS been poured into our hearts through the Holy Spirit, who has been given to us" (Romans 5:5). This love was demonstrated even when you were still living in sin, as Christ, His Son, gave His holy and perfect life for you (5:8). As a believer, you can find peace and hope in the assurance of your salvation, which is a result of your faith. You have been justified by faith and enjoy peace with God in the present (vs. 1, 11). Despite the trials you face in this life (vs. 3-4), you can have a secure hope that God's love and His work for you in Christ and the Spirit will save you from God's wrath on the day of judgment (vs. 5-10) and bring you to glory (vs. 2).

It is amazing! Despite all your flaws and mistakes, God's love can still find a way to bring you back into right standing with Him when you do not deserve it. Indeed, this is "love that surpasses all knowledge" (Eph. 3:19). Also, His love is so great that it can never be fully known, just as the presence and glory of God filled the temple in the (OT) (1 Kg. 8:10-11), so also Paul prays that God would fill the church which you are a member to the full measure of Himself; His presence, moral excellence, power, and love.

"It seems axiomatic to say that it is every human's desire to love and to be loved; indeed, this appears to be the by-product of being created in the community (male and female Gen. 1-2) by the Triune God of love" (Spoelstra 2020, 111).

# His Love for You Is Unselfish

GOD'S LOVE FOR YOU IS UNSELFISH; SCRIPTURE SAYS, "FOR God so loved the world that He gave His one and only Son" for you! (John 3:16). Why? Because Jesus is raised upon the cross and His glorious exaltation (vs. 14-15) is grounded in God's love. God's love is unselfish, not because the world is lovable or because you loved God first. On the contrary, God's love is unselfish because He has a particularly effective selection of love toward His elect (Eph. 5:25). God's love for you is unselfish because it never fails; it never ceases to be a reality. The apostle John penned, "For love comes from God" (1 John. 4:7), this love is unselfish.

Moreover, unselfish love is about giving and sacrificing. Jesus Christ showed the ultimate example of unselfish love when He clothed Himself in humanity. At the same time, He emptied Himself (Kenosis): "His self-emptying was not self-extinction, nor was the divine Being changed into a mere man. In His humanity, He retained the deity consciousness, and His incarnate state carried out the mind that animated Him before His incarnation. He was not unable to assert equality with God. He was able not to assert it"[5] (Vincent 1887, 433).

Likewise, Christ did not cease to be God in the incarnation as if He changed from the form of God into something else. Hence, the Son remained God while also being a man. He added humanity to Himself rather than transforming Himself into a human and humbled Himself when He took your place on the cross.

# His Love for You Is Sacrificial

Not only is God's love for you sacrificial, but it is radical. Jesus was on a mission from the Father. It would require a sacrifice that must be paid in blood that would satisfy the penalty of sin, which is death (Heb. 9:22). Jesus Christ made the ultimate sacrifice by leaving His heavenly dominion because the provisional offerings of the (OT) order on the Day of Atonement (Lev. 16:14-16) were only temporary. According to the law, without the shedding of blood, there is no forgiveness (Lev. 4:7-34, 8:15, 17:11). However, because of Christ's once and final covenant sacrifice, you have been made righteous in the sight of the Father.

When the Father saved you through His Son, His plan and purpose for you took effect. God's presence with you in this world during the lifetime of ministry is the ultimate antidote to fear. The Lord declares, "So do not fear, for I am with you; do not be dismayed, for I am your God. I will strengthen you and help you; I will uphold you with my righteous right hand" (Isa. 41:10). The Father's hand can be trusted to accomplish those things above and beyond all that you will ask according to His will.

"In the Eucharist, crucified and resurrected Christ makes us partake of His permanent state of sacrifice, as eternal High Priest. Out of Christ's pure state of sacrifice we receive the power to offer ourselves to the Father in the Eucharist, together with Him" (Pop 2014, 11).

# His Love for You Is Inseparable

THE APOSTLE PAUL REMINDED THE CHURCH IN ROME, "Neither height nor depth nor anything else in all creation will be able to separate us from the love of God, that is in Christ Jesus our Lord" (Rom. 8:39). You must remember that God will be with you during all your hardships and trails. Paul also penned in his letter to Timothy, "If we died with Him, we will also live with Him; if we endure, we will also reign with Him" (2 Tim. 2:11-12). Following Christ will expose you to persecution, and you must be ready to pay the cost of being a good soldier who is loyal and ready to lay down your life for the gospel of Jesus Christ!

Nevertheless, despite the long-suffering and unselfish commitment, you must realize the blessings and rewards that come to those who endure until the end. God's inseparable love for you will endure forever. However, the carnal mind is not of Christ. If you are not Christ-centered and your interests are not constantly on kingdom-building, the results are spiritual death. "I believe it is one of the devil's ploys in these last days to keep people in a state of perpetual motion."(Buchan 2015, 32).

When your schedule is too busy to keep up with God's plan, you need to rearrange it. Above all, you can be confident that God works in all the circumstances of your life to accomplish His good purpose for you because His love for you is inseparable!

# His Love for You Is Compelling

According to the logos bible word study, the Greek word for "compels" is (ἀγγαρεύω). This means "To behave in a certain way through an injunction" (Faithlife 1992). "For Christ's love compels us" (2 Cor. 5:14). "Christ died for all those who, through faith, embrace God's provision of Salvation. Although only God brought about reconciliation, He appeals to people through His co-workers, such as you " (2 Cor. 5:16-6:2). Jesus is the ultimate example of love, and He demonstrated His love every day, especially when He was conducting His ministry.

"What if a deeper biblical and philosophical analysis of God's character leads us back once again to that simple though this time not simplistic understanding that God is love?" (Kinghorn 2019, 9). Further, His love is compelling due to His willingness not to give up on you! One of my favorite verses proclaims, "But you, Lord, are a compassionate and gracious God, slow to anger, abounding in love and faithfulness" (Ps. 86:15). You must remember that God is faithful "Never will I leave you; never will I forsake you" (Heb. 13:5). The Lord is not in the forsaking business, but he desires to see you living a life that is pleasing to the Father.

Jesus said, "My command is this: Love each other as I have loved you"

(John 15:12). Moreover, this love is displayed supremely in Christ's sacrificial death. It should compel you to want to serve Him, because obedience is not what makes believers Jesus's friends but what characterizes Jesus's friends.

# God Is Not Done with You

Even if you have lost all your worldly possessions, know that God is still with you, and He will restore everything you have lost and return it to you, maybe even (10-fold). One of the most outstanding examples of this in the Scriptures is the story of Job. According to Scripture, Job, Noah, and Daniel are said to constitute the three most righteous men of all time (Ezek. 14:14,20). The three are said to be (1) blameless and (2) upright, having personal integrity and acting justly; however, this does not mean they were sinless. Nevertheless, each man feared God and shunned evil; they were genuinely devoted to God and avoided evil deeds (Job. 28:28).

Indeed, you must do the same; if you do, you will always be favored by God and lacking nothing. I am speaking from experience; I lost everything and was homeless on two separate occasions in the past. I took my eye off the prize, Jesus Christ, and I did not keep my faith despite my circumstances. Eventually, I came to my senses and repented; God restored me on both occasions, which I will get into more detail in the next chapter. Remember, as the apostle Paul wrote in his letter to the Galatians, "Let us not become weary in doing good, for at the proper time we will reap a harvest if we do not give up" (Gal. 6:9). This is a powerful reminder of the rewards of perseverance in faith that you must follow.

Therefore, whether you are currently active in ministry, you may want to give up, throw in the towel, or call it quits. Please do not do it! This is precisely what the enemy wants you to do (John. 10:10). Instead, stand firm and press your way through with the power of prayer. Also, if you were in ministry and walked away as I did, repent, and come back prodigal brother or sister into the ministry, God will restore you because "you were bought with a price" (1 Cor. 6:20) and serve the God of second chances.

# Chapter Five

# The Early Years

LIKE MOST NEW CONVERTS, I CAME INTO THE GOSPEL MINISTRY on fire! I had to tell someone/anyone about my profound encounter with the Person of the Holy Spirit. It was a moment of divine revelation, a spiritual awakening that transformed my life. I started with family members and close friends, at first, they did not believe me; and I did not blame them because they were only going on what I was like prior to my conversion. However, in time they began to see the change that I spoke of whenever they would see me. For this reason, we must live a lifestyle that reflects what is written in the Scriptures. (1 Peter. 1:14-19).

For this reason, it did not take long to go out into the community and witness to whoever would listen to me, whether in the marketplace or on the street, where I would share the gospel with others. My grandfather, who was my pastor then, saw my passion for the lost and my dedication to ministry, so he began to groom me as one of his associate pastors. I received my preaching license the following year, which opened new ministry opportunities only after that. One of my first appointments was as a Sunday school teacher because my grandfather also observed that I had a hunger and thirst for the Word of God. I became a devoted student of the bible. I studied daily and prayed, and the more I repeated the two, the closer I got to God.

Two years passed, and I became trendy within the church and community. Also, I received my Ordination to preach the gospel and started an outreach ministry. I worked with church members and various ministries in the community to evangelize the city of Milwaukee, WI, where I was born and raised. As a result, many came to know Jesus Christ as personal Savior, including family members. Further, over the next few years, I became even more popular in the city and worked with many pastors on various outreach and evangelism projects.

One day, the lord came to me and gave me a vision for a ministry; He gave me a vision and the name that I would call the ministry. Indeed, I was excited that God had chosen me to start a ministry, and I was all in. I devoted much of my time to planning and praying, gathering people and resources for the start-up. However, I was unprepared for what God would teach me and what most believers experience when they are called to start a ministry. We must first learn patience; God's timing and our perception of time are different.

The Scriptures proclaim, "There is a time for everything and a season for every activity under the heavens" (Ecc. 3:4). The teacher in this poem says that every activity has its proper time by God's ordering of the creation. Moreover, apart from birth and death, every activity is one that we have some control over. The problem is that God has set eternity in the human heart; therefore, every person wants to know the big story of which we are a part. However, we are limited and lack the necessary knowledge of the beginning and end to know the time for everything. Indeed, this is where we make errors when it comes to timing.

Therefore, it should not come as a surprise when I tell you that I began to get very weary and frustrated when things did not happen according to my timetable. As time passed, I felt defeated, and God was no longer with me. Note that this is one of the tricks of the enemy, to make you think you are alone, but the bible says, "The Lord Himself goes before you and will be with you; He will never leave you. Do not be afraid; do not be discouraged" (Deut. 31:8). I did not understand that although God gave me the vision, it was not the right time, the vision was for the future. God knew that I was not ready and that there were other things in life I had to overcome and accomplish before the vision would come to fruition.

Subsequently, I went deeper and deeper into despair as time went on until, eventually, I found myself missing one Sunday after another. As a result, I slowly reverted to my old self. Inadvertently, this happens when the ministry becomes more about "us" than God, more about our plans than His plans. Ministry should always be done with the idea of advancing God's agenda and not our own. Nevertheless, I stayed in this state of perpetual misery for many years and even found myself homeless on two occasions, as mentioned earlier. I became the prodigal son who left his father's house searching for an inner peace that was already within me.

According to Scripture, this peace transcends all understanding and will guard your hearts and minds in Christ Jesus." (Phi. 4:7). The nearness of the Holy Spirit grounds both your heart and mind; therefore, we do not need to be anxious, and we must also pray because He is close to us (Ps. 34:15).

Further, because of this peace, His love was calling me back to Himself, into His loving arms, and back to the Father's house. I am reminded of the Scripture that says, "Write down the revelation and make it plan on tablets so that a herald may run with it. The revelation awaits an appointed time; it speaks of the end and will not prove false. Through it linger, wait for it; it will certainly come and will not delay" (Hab. 2:2-3). The word (herald) comes from a root in Hebrew that can mean both "to call out" and "to read" also found in (Exod. 24:7, Deut. 17:19, 2 Kgs. 5:7, Jer. 36:6, 8, 10).

The possible meanings are: "So that the one reading the message may run," either in the sense of delivering the message or in a metaphoric sense of running well, living one's life (Isa. 40:31). Admittedly, I was to "wait for it" with patience and expectancy, since the revelation was time sensitive;

according to God's time; however, I did not, and acted in haste which was my downfall. Those were some of the darkest days of my life, "Because the one who doubts is like a wave of the sea, blown and tossed by the wind" (Jas. 1:6).

James is not saying that our prayers will be answered only if we have a perfect faith that never entertains doubt. He condemns the believer trying to serve two masters simultaneously (Matt. 6:24). Unfortunately, I fell into this category when I allowed myself to want the ministry to flourish when I wanted it to, despite what God was saying and trying to do within me at the time. The Lord gradually moves us toward ministry for a reason, "From everyone who has been given much, much will be demanded; and from the one who has been entrusted with much, much more will be asked" (Luke. 12:48). God always knows best!

Indeed, just like the prodigal son, I came to a crossroads in my life one day. When I said to myself, "What are you doing? This is not what the Father has planned for you. All the while, there were moments and times when I felt convicted about how I was living. However, this time was different; it felt like the Holy Spirit began to overwhelm me as I felt God's power and love rain down upon me. The feeling was revitalizing and energizing, so I began to weep and pray for God's forgiveness.

As a result, slowly, I began to build my confidence by studying/praying and fasting for a new beginning. Also, I found myself back at the house of God, where I slowly began to get involved in outreach ministry, where I started my passion. Likewise, I began to preach and teach the Word of God again with a renewed sense of humility and modesty. The Lord God had restored me, and now I was on a new Journey. Shortly after that, I felt the Spirit directing me back to school. At this point, I began my search for a Bible College or Christian university.

After surfing the web for about a week, I came across Liberty University's website. I have covered many schools, but none have yet to catch my attention, such as the Liberty website. The school's vision is to develop Christ-centered men and women with the values, knowledge, and skills essential for impacting the world for Christ. For this reason, I decided to choose Liberty. I want to impact people wherever I go for the Kingdom of God. I just graduated with my (M. Div.) in May of this year with a focus in Theology/Church leadership and on my way to Seminary in January. God is not done with me yet!

# *His Love for Me*

GOD'S LOVE FOR ME IS SHOWN BY THE FACT THAT HE NEVER left or forgot about His promise to keep and protect me. The Scriptures say, "God is our refuge and strength, an ever-present help in trouble" (Psalm. 46:1). The Lord has indeed been by my side, even when I was a wayward child. He keeps me close, never allowing me to roam too far from His Kingdom. The author Ron Block said, "Everything we need for life and godliness is inside us in Christ, waiting to be unpacked by trust and reliance" (Block 2022, 57). Because love, according to Paul, is patient and kind (1 Cor. 13:4), which Christ has already extended to me.

Likewise, He foreknows me out of His love for me, which explains why God acts on my behalf. My confidence for the present time and future glory is rooted in God's sovereign determination to call me into a relationship with Him, preserve me in a relationship, and vindicate me on the day of His coming. The Father chose to initiate a relationship with me before the world was created, according to (Rom. 8:28-30). Therefore, I can be confident that God will complete His work in me and take me to glory.

Although I do not deserve it, the Father has given me life despite my inability always to do what is right. The Father not only enables me, through His Spirit, to feel His love in my heart, but He also powerfully demonstrated His love for me when He sent His one and only Son to die on my behalf. Therefore, the Spirit brings life to me, liberating me from the power of sin and death. Glory Hallelujah!

# His Love for Me Is Divine

THE FATHER'S DIVINE LOVE FOR ME IS ROOTED IN THE HOLY
Spirit, a gift He has given me, and His marvelous plan for my life, which
He administers through His grace. However, I am often left wondering
why God has chosen me for such a time as this: to proclaim His gospel to
people of all backgrounds and walks of life. The Lord has blessed me with
the riches of His glory and empowered me with His spiritual power,
Providing me with infinite wealth and resources.

The Spirit of God, a powerful force, aids me in overcoming the evil of
this world daily. Above all, His dynamic power is not just a distant
concept, but a living reality communicated by the Spirit. The Holy Spirit
is a powerful force that works and resides in me, a testament to His divine
love. "Jesus expresses the desire to share the exchange of life and love
between He and the Father with those who might believe in Him (17:26),
and He indicates that this sharing of divine life transforms Christians and
reveals that the Father loves them even as the Father loves Christ (17:23)"
(Wessling 2020, 1).

Further, Jesus' distinctive way of addressing God the Father (Mark.
14:36) is taken over by believers like you and me, who enjoy a child's rela-

tionship with God through Him. Therefore, the Spirit of God enables us to speak to the Father similarly, crying out "Abba" Father.

# His Love for Me Is Elected

According to Scripture, God knows me and elected or predestined me to be a part of His Kingdom family even before I was conceived. In his letter to the Ephesians, the apostle Paul wrote, "For He chose us in Him before the world's creation to be holy and blameless in His sight. In love, He predestined us for adoption to sonship through Jesus Christ, by His pleasure and will" (Eph. 1:4-5). Moreover, all believers, male and female, who receive the Spirit that brings about adoption (Rom. 8:15, 23) acquire a new status with its accompanying privileges and responsibilities.

My election and redemption are ultimately for God's glory!

"That which has been eternally determined in Jesus Christ is concretely determined for every individual man to the extent that in the form of the witness of Israel and of the Church, it is also addressed to him and applies to him and comes to him, to the extent that in His Word the electing God enters with him into the relationship of Elector to elected, and by His Word makes him an elected man. This is the predestined man of whom the doctrine of predestination must necessarily speak" (Barth 2010, 115).

Further, God claimed me as His inheritance and possession in much the same way He claimed Israel as His possession and heritage in the (OT) (Ex. 19:5, Deut. 4:20, 9:29, 32:9). As a result, emphasizing God's providence and sovereignty over my life. He is not done with me yet! Despite my shortcomings and past mistakes, He still chose me because of His love for me, and there is nothing I did or can do to deserve it; it is by His grace alone.

# His Love for Me Is Covenantal

⟨⟨⟨ ⟩⟩⟩

THE FATHER MADE A COVENANT WITH ME WHEN HE CHOSE ME to become one of His children. For this same reason, God made a covenant with Abraham. Because of it, "All people on earth will be blessed" (Gen. 12:3). "In the Bible, for the most part, a covenant is a kind of treaty; it establishes or formalizes a relationship and spells out the obligations" (Levenson 2016, 5).The theme of God's blessing to the others through Abram later links to the line of descendants traced initially through Isaac and Jacob as mentioned earlier (Gen. 22:18, 26:4, 27:29, 28:14).

However, the fulfillment of all that God promised Abraham in (Gen. 12:1-3) was conditional upon the patriarch's obedience. Hence, having passed the ultimate test of submission to God, Abraham now receives a solemn guarantee confirming that God will complete everything He promised Abraham (Heb. 6:13-18). Indeed, this family line anticipates the coming of a divinely chosen King who will mediate God's blessing to the nations. This divine oath to Abraham is fulfilled in Jesus Christ (Acts. 3:25-26, Gal. 3:16), my Lord and Savior.

Thank God, righteousness comes from faith. Redemption from the law's curse and justification by faith are preconditions for receiving God's blessing. Scripture regards God's promise to Abraham as a final will or testament and insists that it cannot be set aside by Moses's (later) law. Thank you, Lord, for being a God who loves me and keeps His covenant.

# His Love for Me Is Assured

THE ASSURANCE OF GOD'S LOVE FOR ME COMES IN FIVE WAYS:
(1) His assurance of salvation (1 John. 5:11-12). The Lord's assurance of
answered prayer according to His will (John. 16:24). The Father's assurance of victory over life's temptations (1 Cor. 10:13). His assurance of the
forgiveness of my sin's past, present, and future (1 John. 1:9). Also, God's
assurance of His guidance throughout this life (Prov. 3:5-6). God's
promises and assurances flow from His abundant love toward me.

Although there were many days and nights in the past when my life
choices would not demonstrate the lifestyle of one who had assurance, the
Father never stopped loving me and believing in me. "May we, by His
mercy and grace, be given the ability to understand the past, live powerfully in the present, and look to the future with hope, knowing that God
Himself has given us the answers to the questions we so desperately ask"
(Ham 2007, 19). Christian assurance comes out of faith; when I found
myself lacking faith and out of the will of God, I came to my senses just
like the prodigal son. Knowing I had a Father who loved me and was
waiting for me with open arms.

Moreover, this assurance gives me peace and hope for the future and a determination to fulfill God's plan and purpose for my life. Indeed, because of Christ's love and new covenant sacrifice, I can experience this privileged approach to the Father in worship, prayer, and communion with inward genuineness and full confidence.

# God Is Not Done with Me Yet

ALTHOUGH I WAS HOMELESS TWICE AND LOST EVERYTHING, God kept me safe, and no harm came to me. Just like He saved the three Hebrew boys Shadrach, Meshach, and Abednego from the blazing furnace (Dan. 3:16-27), the Lord saved me from destroying myself. When I look back at the self-destructive behavior that I displayed throughout those years, it makes me weep Because of my selfish thoughts and my self-centered ambitions. One of the quickest ways we can fall from God's grace is to take our eyes off Christ and put our agendas before His.

Thank God for His goodness and mercy, which endures forever. The law and its condemnation no longer have authority over me, according to (Rom. 7:1-6). Moreover, I have been crucified with Christ, and I no longer live, but Christ lives in me" (Gal. 3:20) by His Spirit. Christ has justified me through the cross because justification is by grace alone. Jesus' resurrection was my justification; therefore, I am justified with Him. Further, I must continue to live a life worthy of my calling (Eph. 4:1). Despite my shortcomings or disappointments in the past.

Jesus never promised us that this life would be easy, but He did say that we can overcome it "by the blood of the Lamb and by the word of their testimony" (Rev. 12:11). We must keep the faith, and if we do fall, we must get back up and get right with God again!

# Afterword

Ministry is complex, and we, as leaders, face many obstacles daily. The enemy comes in all shapes and sizes; its only purpose is to hinder you and me from fulfilling God's plan and purpose for our lives. If possible, he will use those you love against you, so we must surround ourselves with godly people. Above all, "Let the message of Christ dwell among you richly as you teach and admonish one another with wisdom through psalms, hymns, and songs from the Spirit, singing to God with gratitude in your hearts" (Col. 3:16).

Also, we must maintain our identity. "There are only two places to look. Either you will get your identity vertically, from who you are in Christ, or you will be shopping for it horizontally in situations, experiences, and relationships of your daily life" (Tripp 2012, 17). As leaders and sons/daughters of the "Most High," we have been adopted into His family and must display a lifestyle of godliness as we engage others. In addition, there must be a balance between ministry and family.

As leaders, we are sent out as examples; therefore, the family must take priority over ministry. Stand firm and never waver; the source of our strength is in the realm not of the physical but of the spiritual. "His love for you and me will always remain the same and never change; therefore, be assured we serve a God of second chances" (Parker 2024, 79-80)).

# Bibliography

Barth, Karl. Church Dogmatics: The Doctrine of God §34–35. the Election of God II. 1st ed. Vol. II.5. London: T&T Clark, 2010.

Block, Ron. Abiding Dependence: Living Moment-by-Moment in the Love of God. 1st ed. Chicago: Moody Publishers, 2022.

Buchan, Angus. Walking by Faith: A Daily Devotional. Oxford: Monarch Books, 2015.

DiMarco, Hayley, and Jenny Youngman. A Woman Overwhelmed: Leader Guide: A Bible Study on the Life of Mary, the Mother of Jesus. Nashville, Tennessee: Abingdon Press, 2017.

Erickson, Millard J. Christian Theology. 3rd ed. Grand Rapids, MI: Baker Academic, 2013.

Faithlife Corporation. Logos Bible Software https://www.logos.com, 1992.

Graves, David E. Biblical Archaeology Second Edition: An Introduction with Recent Discoveries That Support the Reliability of the Bible. 2nd ed. Vol. 1, Toronto, Ont.: Electronic Christian Media, 2018.

Ham, Ken. How could a Loving God? 1st ed. Green Forest, Ark: Master Books Inc, 2007.

Kinghorn, Kevin. But What About God's Wrath? The Compelling Love Story of Divine Anger. United States: InterVarsity Press, 2019.

Levenson, Douglas J. The Love of God: Divine Gift, Human Gratitude, and Mutual Faithfulness in Judaism. 1st ed. Vol. 8. Princeton: Princeton University Press, 2016.

Lockyer, Herbert. All the Women of the Bible: The life and times of all the women of the Bible. Zondervan, 1988.

Nielson, Jon, and Daniel M. Doriani. James: Portrait of a Living Faith: A 13-Lesson Study. Phillipsburg, New Jersey: P & R Publishing, 2019.

Parker, Terry W. His Love for You and His Love for Me: The God of Second Chances. Boynton Beach, FL: Spines Publishing, 2024.

Pop, Irineu. "The Holy Eucharist-Source of Sanctifying Power and Sacrificial Love for God." Facultatea de Teologie Ortodoxă Alba Iulia, no. 1(2014): 7-22.

Rubio, Sarah P. and Anastasia Magloire Williams. Her Story, Her Strength: 50 God-Empowered Women of the Bible. 1st ed. Grand Rapids: Zonderkidz, 2023.

Sampley, Paul J. Walking in Love: Moral Progress and Spiritual Growth with the Apostle Paul. Minneapolis, MN: Fortress Press, 2016.

Spoelstra, Joshua J. God's Love Story: A Canonical Telling. Eugene, Oregon: Wipf & Stock, 2020.

Tripp, David P. Dangerous Calling: Confronting the Unique Challenges of Pastoral Ministry. 1st ed. Wheaton, IL: Crossway, 2012.

Vincent, Richardson M. Word Studies in the New Testament. Vol. 3. New York: Charles Scribner's Sons, 1887.

Wessling, Jordan. Love Divine: A Systematic Account of God's Love for Humanity. First ed. Oxford, United Kingdom; New York: Oxford University Press, 2020.

Whittock, Esther, and Martyn J. Whittock. Daughters of Eve: Women of the Bible. First ed. Oxford, England: Lion Hudson, 2021.

Made in the USA
Middletown, DE
02 September 2024

60257416R00056